Water Wise!

Alison Hawes

Published 2010 by
A & C Black Publishers Ltd.
36 Soho Square, London, W1D 3QY

www.acblack.com

ISBN   HB 978-1-4081-2424-6
       PB 978-1-4081-2687-5

Series consultant: Gill Matthews

Text copyright © 2010 Alison Hawes

This book is produced using paper that is made from wood grown in managed, sustainable forests. It is natural, renewable and recyclable. The logging and manufacturing processes conform to the environmental regulations of the country of origin.

Produced for A & C Black by Calcium. www.calciumcreative.co.uk

Printed and bound in China by C&C Offset Printing Co.

All the internet addresses given in this book were correct at the time of going to press. The author and publishers regret any inconvenience caused if addresses have changed or sites have ceased to exist, but can accept no responsibility for any such changes.

Acknowledgements

The publishers would like to thank the following for their kind permission to reproduce their photographs:

Cover: Shutterstock. **Pages:** Corbis: Gideon Mendel 15, Liba Taylor 18b, Peter Turnley 16b; Dreamstime: Atm2003; Istockphoto: Irina Belousa 21, Claudia Dewald 23b, David Joyner 2–32, Rusm 4–23, Sean Warren 30; Pump Aid: 26t, 26b, 27; Shutterstock: Stefan Ataman 12t, Paul Brennan 11, Lucian Coman 14t, 18t, 20t, FloridaStock 17b, Goldenangel 4b, Khafizov Ivan Harisovich 9t, Michal Kaco 9b, Kkaplin 5t, Andreas G. Karelias 8t, Dmitry Melnikov 6b, Micimakin 28t, Oleg_Z 6t, Olly 8b, Irina Ovchinnikova 14b, 20b, Anton Prado Photo 16t, Alexander Raths 22t, Dr. Morley Read 5b, RTimages 10t, Lloyd Smith 17t, Yves Smolders 24t, Stocklight 7, Thefinalmiracle 10b, Theodor S 4t, Marc van Vuren 12b; WaterAid: Marco Betti 22b, Juthika Howlander 19, Eva-Lotta Jansson 24b, Susanne Porter 23t, Layton Thompson 25, 28c, 28b.

Contents

Water – Why Worry?

If the world's water fitted into a bucket only one teaspoon of it would be drinkable!

Can't live without it?

Water is the most precious **natural resource** on Earth. It is more precious than gold, diamonds, or oil! This is because all living things depend on water to exist. No plant, animal, or human can survive without it. There is no **substitute** for it. Only water will do.

We can live for weeks without food but only days without water.

I don't get it!

But I don't see the problem. Three quarters of the world is covered in water!

That's true, but 97 per cent of that water is *salty*. Just 3 per cent is *fresh* water – and only a tiny part of that is **accessible** to us.

In some parts of the world, people, crops, and animals are dying because of a shortage of water.

Water worries

There is enough water for everyone, but due to lack of rain, money, or **overpopulation**, not everyone is able to get enough of that water for their needs. To make matters worse, the world's population is increasing incredibly quickly, which means that more people have to share the same amount of water.

So shouldn't something be done to sort out the world's water supply, NOW, rather than later?

Water Wasters

Too much!

Did you realise that people who live in water-rich countries are the biggest users and wasters of water in the world?

We each only need about 60 litres (13 gallons) of water a day for **sanitation**, drinking, cooking, and washing. But the truth is we all use much, much more than this. People who live in Europe use about 200 litres (44 gallons) of water per person per day. But in North America, this rises to 400 litres (88 gallons) a day.

If we all remembered to switch off the tap while we were brushing our teeth, millions of litres of water would be saved every year.

Wastage

Part of the reason we each use so much is water is that we do not always use our water wisely. For example, some of us choose to take a bath every day instead of a quick shower.

Do you know, every time you water your garden with a sprinkler you use 800 litres (176 gallons) of water an hour? This is a waste of water.

What can I do, now?

- Think carefully about how you use water at home.
- Try to find ways to save or recycle water every day.

Heavy Users

The water we use at home is actually very small when compared to the vast quantities used by industry and agriculture.

Industry

Almost everything we buy is made using water. Either water is part of what is being made, like in beer and tinned food; or water is used for washing or cooling what is being made. Also, industries are often big polluters of water.

In some countries, such as Russia, pollution from factories has found its way into the drinking water.

Many factories take water from our rivers and then return the used, polluted water back to the water supply. Isn't that worrying?

Some sprinkler systems waste enormous amounts of water.

Agriculture

By far the biggest users of water in the world are farmers. Do you realize that it takes about 1,000 litres (220 gallons) of water just to produce one kilo (2 lbs) of potatoes?

The agricultural industry is also sometimes guilty of polluting the water supply with the **fertilizers** and **pesticides** they use.

What can I do, now?

- Support groups trying to clean up your local environment.
- Write to the government. Ask them to introduce tougher anti-pollution laws.

Enough Water?

Instant access

Think about it, you can turn on a tap whenever you need water. You always have enough water to drink. You don't have to walk miles to fetch and carry water. Many people in water-poor countries have to do this EVERY day.

Many women and children spend up to a quarter of their day fetching water.

Water shortages

Often water-rich countries pump more water out of the ground than can be replaced by rain. Many parts of the world, such as California, Italy, and the UK, have had water shortages in the past few years.

Over building

Water shortages are not helped by the amount of building taking place in water-rich countries. More homes, towns, and cities being built cover the soil with concrete. This means less rainwater is able to flow back into the ground to refill our underground lakes (or aquifers). We rely on these for much of our water supply.

We think nothing of taking our cars through a car wash. This wastes huge amounts of water, when many people in the world do not have enough water to drink.

What can I do, now?

- Ask your parents not to pave over your garden.
- Don't use tap water on your gardens.
- Write to the government. Ask them to repair and use old buildings before building new ones.

Water Losers

Millions of people across the world do not have enough clean freshwater for their needs. Does this sound fair to you?

Rainfall

All countries need rain to top up the **reservoirs**, rivers, and underground lakes that they take their water from. But some countries get hardly any rain at all, while some places get too much.

Flooding

Too much rain at once can cause flooding. Flood water is not drinkable and can often carry deadly diseases, like **cholera**.

Parts of the world, particularly Asia, regularly experience severe flooding.

Poor access

Even when a country has enough rain, it does not always have the reservoirs, pumping stations, and water pipes it needs. These bring clean, safe water to everyone's home. Sometimes, this is because the government cannot or will not pay for these things. This means that millions of people often live a long way from a source of fresh water.

Some people have no choice but to collect and drink unsafe water.

What can I do, now?

- Support an organization like UNICEF that helps people in water-poor countries improve their access to fresh water.
- Raise money for a water charity like WaterAid that helps water-poor countries with their water needs.

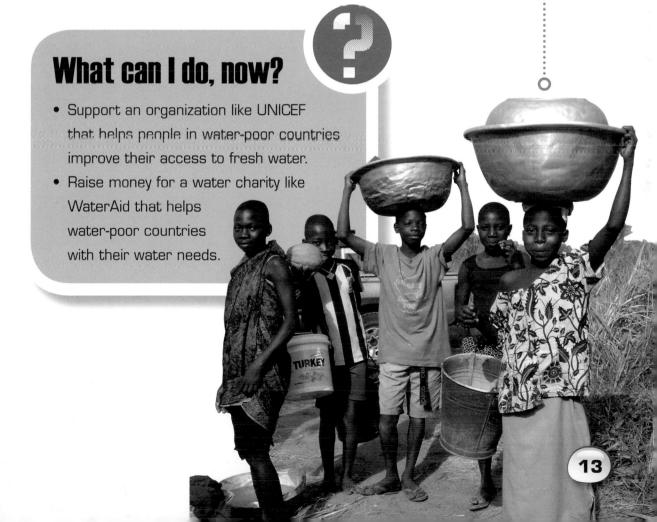

Dirty Water

Good sanitation

In your home you have toilets that flush. You have sinks, baths, and showers to use for washing. There are also pipes that take away **sewage** and dirty water from your homes and schools. In fact, you do not have to think twice about having enough water, or **facilities**, to wash or go to the toilet. But for billions of other people life is quite different.

Children who live and play near dirty water are often ill.

In water-poor countries, diarrhoea is a very serious illness. Billions of people suffer from it and millions of people, especially children, die from it.

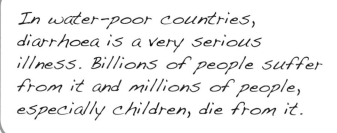

Poor sanitation

Sadly, water-poor countries often have poor sanitation too. About 2.6 billion people are living day after day without proper facilities.

Just stop and think!

What does living without proper sanitation really mean? It could mean not having a bathroom or enough water to wash with. It could mean not having a proper toilet or pipes to take the dirty water away from your home. It could even mean not having a toilet at all.

Can you imagine having to try and find somewhere private outside every time you need to go to the toilet?

Future Losers?

What might the world be like if the water-rich countries carry on using water carelessly?

Less food and water

If we do nothing, water-poor countries will have less water than they do now. Populations are still growing, which means there will be more people to share the water and more people to feed – but not enough water for everyone to grow food.

Severe food shortages lead to famine.

More disease

In poor countries, where people are already dying from diseases spread by dirty water and poor sanitation, more and more people will die. Illnesses like cholera and **typhoid** will continue to spread.

Nearly 2 million children die each year because of dirty water and poor sanitation.

Less wildlife

As water becomes more polluted, more and more birds and animals will die. As water is drained from wet areas through activities such as building dams, more and more wildlife will die through loss of habitat.

Future Winners?

The world could be very different, if only we were to take better care of the world's water now and in the future.

Working together

In an ideal world, all the countries in the world would work together to improve access to water in some parts of the world and save water in others.

Millions of people would no longer suffer from deadly diseases.

Improving access

People in water-poor countries would have the money and resources to access clean water and good sanitation. Countries that use the same water supply would agree to share and not argue, as some countries are doing right now.

What can I do, now?

- Reduce and recycle as much water as possible.
- Ask your parents to replace old washing machines, dishwashers, showers, and toilets with ones that use less water.

Improved sanitation makes a big difference to people's health and happiness.

Who is helping?

Millions still need help

Many governments and international organizations are working hard right now to improve access to clean water for many of the poorest people in the world. This is good news for those who have been helped. But what about the millions of others who still lack a safe water supply?

Why don't you write to your government? Encourage them to support more projects in water-poor countries. Try and make them see that what is already being done needs to be done faster!

A simple water pump can improve the health and wealth of poor people.

Raise money, raise aid

Many water charities are currently helping water-poor countries, but charities have to rely on money from us to carry out their work. So why not help to raise money for them? Remember, the more money you raise, the more people can be helped.

Desalination plants can turn seawater into drinking water, but this costs a lot of money.

New technologies

- Some countries, such as the USA and Saudi Arabia, are turning seawater into freshwater.

- China and the USA are using **cloud seeding** to produce more rain in dry areas of their country.

Cleaning Up

Dignity and privacy

When a school has no toilet, children have to go to the toilet in a bush. As you can imagine, this is not private or dignified. It also means the children can be in danger from wild animals and insects. In schools without water and sanitation, teachers and children frequently fall sick — and schools often close. The **installation** of toilets changes all that.

This school in India now has clean and private toilets.

Every 15 seconds a child dies from a water-related disease.

Learning to keep clean

Health education is given to adults and children to teach them the importance of keeping clean and washing hands. They also learn that doing this stops the spread of disease. Many schools don't have access to books or pictures, but the children get to know about **hygiene** by learning songs and performing plays.

A local teacher talks to children about how to keep clean and healthy.

Healthy people are happy people

Access to good sanitation and health education are equally as important as access to clean water. Having these three things means people can lead happier, healthier lives. WaterAid and Pump Aid are just two charities working to achieve these goals.

WaterAid

WaterAid is a water charity that hopes one day to see everyone in the world having a safe water supply and good water facilities.

In 2008/09, WaterAid helped 1.14 million people gain access to safe water and millions more to improve their sanitation.

With the charity's help, these people laid water pipes to bring clean water to their village.

Working locally

WaterAid works on water and sanitation projects in 17 different countries in Africa, Asia, and the Pacific region. In these countries, they involve local people in building and looking after their own wells, water pumps, water pipes, and toilets.

Helping the poorest

WaterAid tries to persuade governments around the world of the importance of clean water and sanitation. They also encourage governments to spend more of their money on improving water supplies to the poorest people in their country. They believe that improving water supplies for these people is the first step to solving world **poverty**.

A water pump in a village often means there is enough water to grow vegetables. This gives villagers a greater variety of food to eat and also means any extra vegetables can be sold to earn money.

What can I do, now?

- Support a water charity.

Pump Aid

Pump Aid is a water charity working in Africa. They mostly help people to build water pumps and toilets at their schools and near their homes.

Elephant pumps

Pump Aid's water pumps are specially designed so that they are cheap and easy to build by local people, using local materials. They are also easy for local people to **maintain** and repair.

Even very young children can use Elephant pumps.

Pump Aid water pumps give people quick and easy access to clean water.

Elephant toilets

Pump Aid's award-winning Elephant toilets are designed to provide private, clean, and safe toilets for people to use.

Like an elephant!

Elephant pumps and toilets are so-called because they look a little like an elephant. The handles of Elephant pumps look like ears and the pipe looks like a trunk! Elephant toilets have two ear-like shapes in the ground in which you place your feet, and a long, trunk-like hole that carries away waste.

What can I do, now?

- Get together with some friends and raise enough money to build an Elephant toilet.

?

Elephant toilets provide good sanitation – and privacy.

27

Get Water Wise!

Save water

We can all save water by being water wise at home, school, and work.

Find out how you can help WaterAid raise money at: www.wateraid.org.uk

Donate your old mobile phone to WaterAid to help them raise money.

Look at this table. How many of these water saving tips have you and your family tried?

Water saving tip	Notes	Water saved
Turn off the tap when brushing your teeth	Use a mug of water instead	6 litres (just over 1 gallon) a minute
Put a water saving pack in your toilet cistern	You can get a water saving pack or "hippo" from many water companies	1–3 litres (up to ½ a gallon) a flush
Have a shower instead of a deep bath	Power showers use a lot of water, so if you've got one, make sure you have a quick shower	60 litres (13 gallons) a time
Turn off the tap! A dripping or running tap is a waste of water	Teachers sometimes find children have left taps running at school	10 litres (over 2 gallons) or more a day.
Don't use tap water in the garden	Collect rainwater in a water butt. Use a watering can, instead of a hose or sprinkler	Up to 800 litres (176 gallons) an hour

Remember! We can all do something to help manage the world's water more wisely. One person might not make a lot of difference but if we all work together we can make a BIG difference.

Glossary

accessible easily available, reachable or useable

cloud seeding shooting or dropping chemicals like silver iodide into clouds to make them produce more rain.

cholera an infectious disease of the intestines

facilities equipment

fertilizer something added to soil to make grow plants grow well

hygiene rules or ways to keep healthy

installation to fit or put something into place

maintain keep in good repair

natural resource something useful or valuable that occurs naturally, not artificially made

overpopulation too many people living in one place

pesticide something that kills insects that damage plants

poverty being poor

reservoir a man made or natural lake used as a water supply

sanitation the disposal of sewage and rubbish from homes

sewage dirty water, toilet waste

substitute replacement

typhoid a serious infectious disease

Further Information

Websites

For video clips and more info about Pump Aid's work, go to:
www.pumpaid.org

For games and personal stories from people helped by WaterAid and to hear The Poo Song!, go to the Learn Zone at:
www.wateraid.org

For information about children who live in countries helped by UNICEF go to:
www.unicef.org.uk

Books

Can the Earth Cope? – Water Supply by Louise Spilsbury. Wayland (2008).

You Can Save the Planet by R Hough. A & C Black (2007).

How We Use and Abuse Water by P Grant and A. Haswell. Belitha Press (2000).

Index